MI MUSICIANS INSTITUTE

MASTER CLASS

Classical & Fingerstyle
Guitar Techniques

by David Oakes

ISBN 0-7935-8045-5

HAL•LEONARD®
CORPORATION
7777 W. BLUEMOUND RD. P.O. BOX 13819 MILWAUKEE, WI 53213

Visit Hal Leonard Online at
www.halleonard.com

GW01454346

Introduction

Who Should Use This Book?

This book is aimed at any guitarist who wants a quick, thorough grounding in the essentials of classical and fingerstyle guitar technique. This book was not written as a method for beginning guitarists, however, nor do I regard it as a complete classical/fingerstyle guitar method. I have taught at Musicians Institute for the past twelve years, and during this time have exposed hundreds of players to the world of classical and fingerstyle guitar. Most of the students I work with have anywhere from three to ten years experience in every conceivable style—except classical guitar. These materials have been developed to meet the needs of such an electric or acoustic guitarist.

How Does It Work?

The first step in learning to play classical/fingerstyle guitar is to build technique in the right and left hands—by developing relaxation, awareness, and finger independence. Therefore, this book is divided into lessons, and each lesson works on a specific technique for the right and/or left hand. Each technique will be broken down into very simple movements that can be learned quickly, and the movements will then be placed into the context of a study, or étude, so that the technique can be reinforced.

The right hand will focus on two specific techniques:

- **free stroke**—used primarily when playing chords and arpeggios.
- **rest stroke**—used to bring out melodies in an arrangement, and when playing single-note passages.

The left hand, meanwhile, will focus on developing the general strength, relaxation, and finger independence needed to play more than one part at a time. The lessons will go into these techniques in great detail.

In addition to these classical techniques, this book also includes lessons on thumb independence, thumb-and-index scale technique, three-to-a-string patterns, and rasqueado—making it a valuable reference for other fingerstyle genres like jazz, country, and flamenco.

Where Do I Start?

This material can be used in a variety of different ways. The core of it is the technique. If your interest is primarily in fingerstyle playing, you can work on the techniques and, for the most part, skip over the classically oriented études. For practice, I'd suggest you compose your own song or guitar composition with each technique, or apply it to an existing song's accompaniment. If you want to learn how to play fingerstyle guitar and use classical technique to get started, then work on all the techniques and a few of the études, as you see fit. (You can also substitute popular fingerstyle guitar music for many of the classical études.) If, on the other hand, classical guitar is your passion, then go through everything in this book, and don't skip a note!

My experience has shown that it generally takes a student one week to learn and begin to internalize a technique. From this point, you should spend another one to two weeks on the étude before moving on to the next section. If it takes you a little longer, or a little shorter, that's fine. Be patient, and enjoy your progress as it comes.

Onward!

—David Oakes

Table of Contents

Holding the Classical Guitar

Standard Position

The standard method for holding the classical guitar is to place it across the left leg and, using a footstool, elevate the leg to a point where the guitar is at an approximately 30 degree angle to the player. There are several reasons why classical guitarists sit this way:

- It lets the guitar rest against your chest and legs, leaving both arms free to move (without having to exert extra pressure and tension to hold the instrument).
- The guitar is placed in a position that will project the sound acoustically to the back of the room.

These are very important considerations. However, most guitarists who have learned to play without this position find this method of sitting very uncomfortable. Furthermore, many doctors, chiropractors, and experts in ergonomics say that this sitting position places stress on the lower back and weakens the body's musculoskeletal system.

The 90 Degree Rule

My sitting position uses one concept: *the 90 degree rule.* Your feet should be flat on the floor. Your knees should be at a 90 degree angle to your feet. Your legs should be bent at a 90 degree angle at your knees. Your trunk should be at a 90 degree angle to your legs, bent at your hips. Your back should be straight, and your shoulders parallel to the ground. Then I like to use items such as an A-frame stand or a cushion to prop the guitar up on the left leg. This is a position that will give your body more strength.

Another item that I use quite often is a guitar strap. Of course, I don't use a strap with an expensive classical guitar, but on cheaper guitars I have found it very useful. In pit orchestra situations, a strap is often practical because of space considerations. In the classroom, I am constantly walking around the room with my guitar to help students. I often use a strap when I am playing gigs. In more formal classical guitar performances, I will use the A-frame guitar stand positioned on my left leg.

NOTE: Sitting for long periods, even in the above position, can tire out the back. To counter this, I like to sit in a chair that has a forward slope. If the chair doesn't have slope, I use a wedge cushion to sit on. Other alternatives would be to roll up a towel at the back of the seat or to place a 2" x 4" piece of wood under the back legs of the chair. This can greatly reduce any tension that might build up in your back; it will also allow you to lean forward without feeling like you are slumping over the guitar.

Alternate Positions

1. **A variation on standard:** The footstool is higher, and the guitar is resting on the knee in a different location. This places the instrument a little more to the player's right side, which will help many players feel more comfortable. The guitar is in a similar position as a guitar strap holding the instrument.

2. **Traditional flamenco sitting position:** The flamenco guitar I am using in the photo is very light in construction. I could also use my chin to help balance the instrument if I wanted to.

3. **A more contemporary flamenco position:** A favorite among guitarists of all styles. This position helps relieve stress in my back and shoulders. I use it for short periods of time everyday, but I try not to spend too much time here, and I don't recommend using this as your normal sitting position.

Hand Position

As I expect you to have some playing experience already and, therefore, your own habits and preferences, my rules for hand position are minimal:

- Try to keep the hand, wrist, and forearm in a straight line. This correctly aligns the muscles and relaxes the hand position. Relaxation will develop only with correct muscle alignment. This applies to both hands.
- Make sure you can see the knuckles in both hands when you play. To do this, you'll need to have a uniform curve in each finger. Each hand needs to be in a neutral (midrange) position; bending the wrist on either hand tends to flex or extend the muscles, which will inhibit your playing technique.
- Try to keep your left hand moving parallel to the fingerboard, with your left-hand thumb on or near the center of the guitar neck, in line between the index and middle fingers.

Practice in front of a mirror during the first few months of playing the classical guitar so that you can visually check your hand positions and posture. Once these techniques feel comfortable and are internalized, lose the mirror.

Fingernails

Too much emphasis gets placed on right-hand fingernail shape when people are starting to play classical or fingerstyle guitar. I think that it is much more important to learn to play from the tip of the finger and get a very quick release off of the string when plucking (without the nail), and then add a small amount of fingernail to support the sound as your playing progresses. Many guitarists will grow long fingernails and gradually lose all contact with the fingertip when plucking a string. My point is that you need to take time to get your right-hand attack consistent and relaxed, and then add fingernails. This will take anywhere from three to six months.

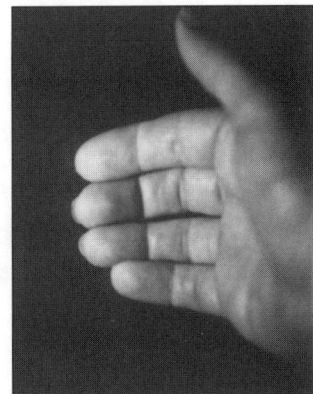

Classical Guitar Notation

Classical guitar music often includes both right- and left-hand fingerings in its notation. These are a little awkward to read at first, but with a little practice, your eyes will adjust to reading and learning the fingerings along with the notes.

Left-Hand Fingerings

The numbers above, below, or to the left of a notehead refer to the left-hand fingering. Sometimes, when an accidental is attached to a note, the fingering is to the right of the notehead.

1 = index finger   3 = ring finger
2 = middle finger   4 = pinky finger

Strings and Frets

The circled numbers ①②③④⑤⑥ refer to the strings on which a note should be played. ① is the first, or high E string, and ⑥ is the sixth, or low E string.

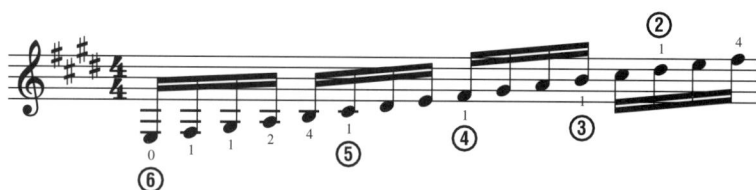

The letter "B" followed by a Roman numeral refers to fretboard position. For example, "BIV" means "barre at the fourth fret." Technically, B stands for "barre," but barre only if you need to. In other publications, the letter C (*ceja,* or capo) is used for the same indication.

Right-Hand Fingerings

The letters *p, i, m,* and *a* directly below a notehead refer to the right-hand fingering. These letters are derived from the Spanish names for the fingers. (Remember, the guitar is a Spanish instrument.)

p = thumb (pulgar)   *m* = middle (medio)
i = index (indice)   *a* = ring (annular)

About the Tablature in This Book

Tablature has been included in this book for those players with little or no music reading experience who simply want a grounding in classical guitar technique. As a guitarist, I do not care for tablature: Written music is a language that we share with every other instrument, and we need to be able to speak that language to effectively communicate with other musicians—to read, write, play, *and* improvise.

If you have any experience in note-reading, then you should completely ignore the tablature. There is more than enough fingering information written into the staff notation. If you must, refer to the tablature for an occasional fret location, but when you practice an étude, always look at the notes on the staff, especially for fingering information.

If you don't know how to read music, I strongly encourage you to learn!

Lesson 1

RIGHT HAND
Finding Your Hand Position

This first exercise develops awareness and teaches you how to find a correct playing position for your right hand. This is a simple yet very important exercise, so don't overlook it:

Rest your right forearm lightly on the top side of the guitar. Don't let the elbow touch the top or sides of the instrument. Try to keep your forearm and wrist in line with each other, as straight as possible. People over 5' 9" will probably have to bend the wrist down slightly because of their longer arms. The wrist should be about three to four inches above the top of the guitar. Many people keep their wrist low because of their right-hand flat-picking technique; however, in fingerstyle guitar, the wrist needs to be higher to get more power when you pluck the strings.

Next, place your index finger on the third string, your middle finger on the second string, and your ring finger on the first string. Place your thumb on the fifth string. Check your hand position. The right-hand finger joints should be in a midrange or neutral position. Many people will extend their ring finger while keeping the index and middle fingers curved. Try to keep a uniform curve in each finger joint.

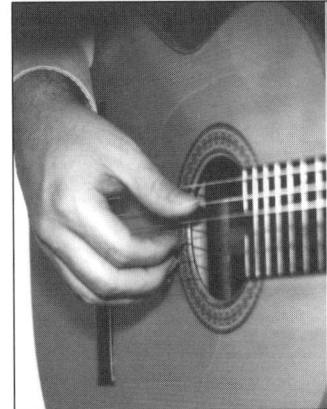

You will probably need to spend a few moments each day getting comfortable with this hand position. I suggest that you practice holding this position while feeling the strings on the tips of your fingers for several minutes each day, for a week or two.

Free Stroke: Playing from the String

By far the most common technique in classical and fingerstyle guitar is the *free stroke*. (It's particularly useful in playing chords and arpeggios, as we'll see in the next lessons.) There are different schools of thought on how to execute the free stroke; we'll use the concept of *playing from the string* (also called "planting"). The fingers of your right hand actually touch the string an instant before they pluck. This will seem very awkward at first, but there are many advantages to developing this technique:

- It will stabilize your right hand, making your hand positions very relaxed.
- It will help you develop better tone production and make your attack very consistent.
- It will allow you to develop more speed and fluency in your playing.

As before, place **(touch)** the index finger on the third string, the middle finger on the second string, and the ring finger on the first string. Place the thumb on the fifth string. Now, with the index finger on the third string, **relax** the tip segment of the finger. Different people have different levels of flexibility in the tip segments of their fingers; you just want to flex a little in the tip segment. This helps to absorb the shock of the string when the finger plucks and will provide a very quick release off of the string. Finally, **pluck** the string from the top knuckle of the index finger, and follow through under the palm of your hand as if you were making a relaxed fist in your hand.

touch

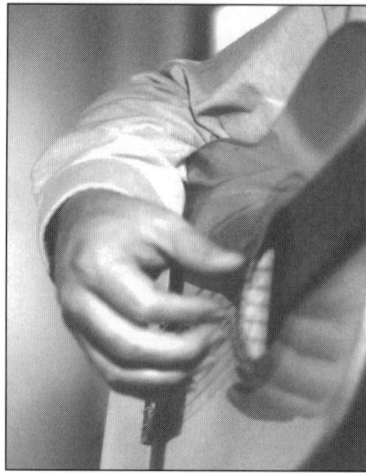

relax

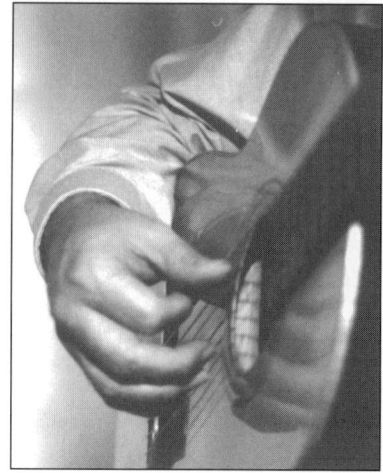

pluck

I also call this the "touch-relax-pluck" method—for obvious reasons. Don't exaggerate the follow-through after you have plucked the string. Continue the exercise with all the finger combinations below. When plucking a free stroke with the thumb, again pluck from the top knuckle (the knuckle that connects the thumb to the hand), and follow through with a smooth motion that moves towards the index finger.

The touch-relax-pluck exercise is not the way we play the guitar, per se, but it will help you develop proper awareness, relaxation, powerful attack, and incredible finger independence. Watch out for these common technique mistakes:

- Many people tend to play the free stroke from the middle knuckle. This creates a lot of tension in your right hand and greatly reduces tone production.
- The thumb also tends to bend at the middle knuckle. Many pickstyle guitarists play with a bent thumb, and this makes it difficult to change. It is alright for the thumb to bend backwards in the opposite direction. (If you look at pictures of classical guitarists, they will have either a straight thumb—à la John Williams—or a bent back thumb—à la Andres Segovia.)
- When you play the double stops in exercises 4–6, work to achieve even tone production between each finger.
- Keep the fingers and thumb that aren't playing lightly relaxed on their respective strings. This will be very difficult at first, especially with the index-and-ring-finger combination. With practice, you will develop the independence and relaxation to do this.

For the first two weeks, try to practice this exercise twice a day for about five minutes each practice session. This exercise should be the first thing you do when you pick the guitar up and the last thing you do when you put it away—five minutes, two times per day. During this practice session, take time to place the fingers correctly, and then take time to judge your attack. It is very important that over the course of the week of your practice you develop consistency and relaxation with your right-hand free stroke attack.

I would also suggest beginning your practice sessions with this exercise for about three months. This will help you to focus your attention on your right-hand attack before practicing other techniques in this book. When you feel that this exercise is mastered, then it is time to add a little fingernail to support the attack.

About the CD

Starting with Lesson 2, every example in this book is played on the accompanying CD. The tempos selected for the recording are moderate, but fast enough that you can hear the general flow of the music and phrasing. I would suggest that you first practice the exercises slower than they are performed on the CD, but work up your tempos gradually over the period of two to three weeks that you spend with each lesson. Some of the examples—the harmonics in Lesson 11, for instance—are to be played "out of time," in a rubato fashion. The count-offs just let you know when I begin playing. Throughout the CD, I have occasionally left out repeats in order to save time, but you should practice these repeats on your own. In Lesson 12, I repeat each of the one-bar rasgueado examples three times each, sometimes varying the rhythm of the strums; listen to these examples carefully.

LEFT HAND
The Supported Finger Exercise

Playing classical and fingerstyle guitar requires considerable left-hand finger independence—a strong but relaxed left-hand position is essential to smooth chord changes and legato single-note lines. This is a great exercise for developing left-hand finger independence while also keeping the hand very relaxed. The object is to move one left-hand finger at a time across the strings, while the other fingers remain resting lightly *(supportive fingering)* along a middle string:

Begin in the fifth position (i.e., at the fifth fret), with your left-hand fingers resting on the third string. The fingers that are not moving (shown with white dots) should be resting lightly, but not actually pushing the third string down. Keep your focus on the finger that is moving (shown with black dots), and don't think too much about the fingers that are supporting the move.

Let your fingers move slowly and with precision. Concentrate on the motion, and direct each movement. This exercise will help your playing become smoother and more connected.

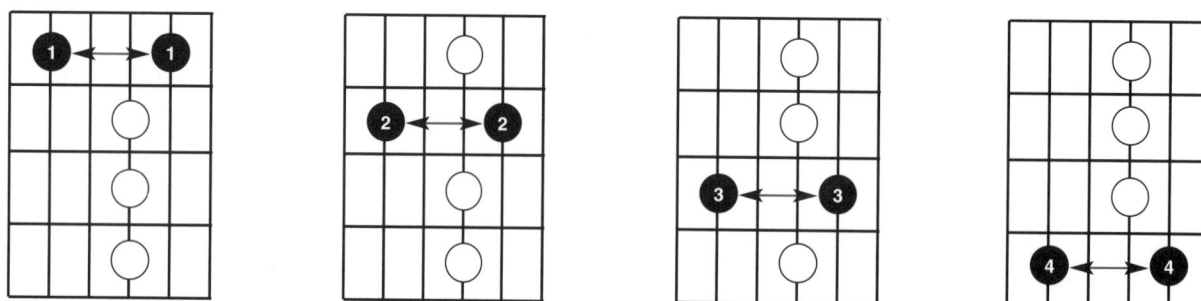

Be aware of your left-hand position during this exercise:

- The left hand and wrist are not bent; they are a natural extension of the forearm.
- The thumb should be exerting very little pressure on the back of the neck. Relax!
- The hand should be parallel to the fingerboard. The first and fourth fingers play on the sides of the fingers while the second and third fingers are on the fingertips. The stretch from the fingers comes from the knuckles at the hand. (You should be able to see the knuckles.)

This exercise can be practiced moving up and down the fingerboard, or you can choose to keep it in one position. It should be practiced for approximately five minutes each day for two weeks.

Lesson 2
RIGHT HAND
Forward Arpeggios

Now that we've learned the correct preparation of the free stroke, as well as the correct attack and follow-through, let's concentrate on applying these techniques to *forward arpeggios*. An *arpeggio* is the notes of a chord, played one at a time. In a forward arpeggio, the thumb plucks a bass string and is followed by any combination of the index, middle, and ring fingers in an ascending movement.

Play the following forward arpeggios using your free stroke technique—i.e., playing from the string. Practice slowly: This will give you time to check your attack. Make sure that your fingers touch the string and rest there for an instant before you pluck the string, and then get a quick release off each string. Remember, you should be slightly relaxing the tip segment of your fingertips as you pluck the string and allowing a natural follow-through of each finger.

Frequently asked questions or thoughts about "playing from the string":

- Many guitarists don't like this technique at first because it cuts off the sound of the notes. To avoid this problem, make sure that you're not placing the fingers too far in advance. Remember, the finger will touch the string and rest there just an instant before it plucks.

- There will be times when the top note of the arpeggio will need to sustain. In these cases, don't touch the string before you pluck it.

- Initially, it can be awkward to learn to play arpeggios this way. Remember: you are still learning to play from the string and to prepare your fingers in advance. Give yourself some time, and make the effort to develop this technique.

In the long run, this is a great way to practice arpeggios. You'll make less mistakes because your fingers are preparing to play in advance, you'll develop an even attack and consistent tone, and you'll build confidence and incredible speed.

As with other techniques in this book, it should take you about a week or two to begin to internalize this technique, spending about 30 minutes per day. When you're ready, begin practicing the following study—slowly. Allow yourself one to two more weeks on the study before moving on to the next lesson.

5 Caprice in C (excerpt)

Matteo Carcassi
(1792-1853)

Lesson 3
RIGHT HAND
Reverse Arpeggios

We've learned how to play forward arpeggios, but music tends to go in the other direction as well. In *reverse arpeggios,* the thumb plucks a bass note and is then followed by any combination of the ring, middle, and index fingers in a *descending* movement. The technique of finger preparation is essentially the same.

Practice slowly, but with very quick movements. Remember that each finger touches the string and rests there just an instant before playing. This must become subconscious when you perform arpeggio passages.

When playing arpeggios—forward or reverse—a very important principle is to have each finger at a different point in its cycle. While one finger plucks and follows through, another finger is returning to the string that it plays next, and another finger is touching the string that it is about to play (cycling). This next arpeggio is an excellent example on which to practice this concept.

We've all heard the saying "Practice makes perfect." I think that practice makes permanent, not perfect. Our brains are just as capable of memorizing poor hand positions, bad technique, sloppy playing, bad tone, and wrong notes as they are of memorizing the correct notes and relaxed hand positions. When you first start practicing a new technique or music, your brain is memorizing every little detail. As you continue practicing, your brain will become tired of slaving over the details of the technique and will give the job over to "the motor strip." The motor strip is much better at carrying out the details at faster tempos.

With this in mind, why would anyone want to try and force learning a technique incorrectly or poorly by practicing too fast? Give whatever you're practicing time, and let your tempos increase naturally. The amount of time is different for everyone. You will start feeling more and more comfortable with the technique, and the speed will just develop.

9 Prelude in C

Fernando Carulli

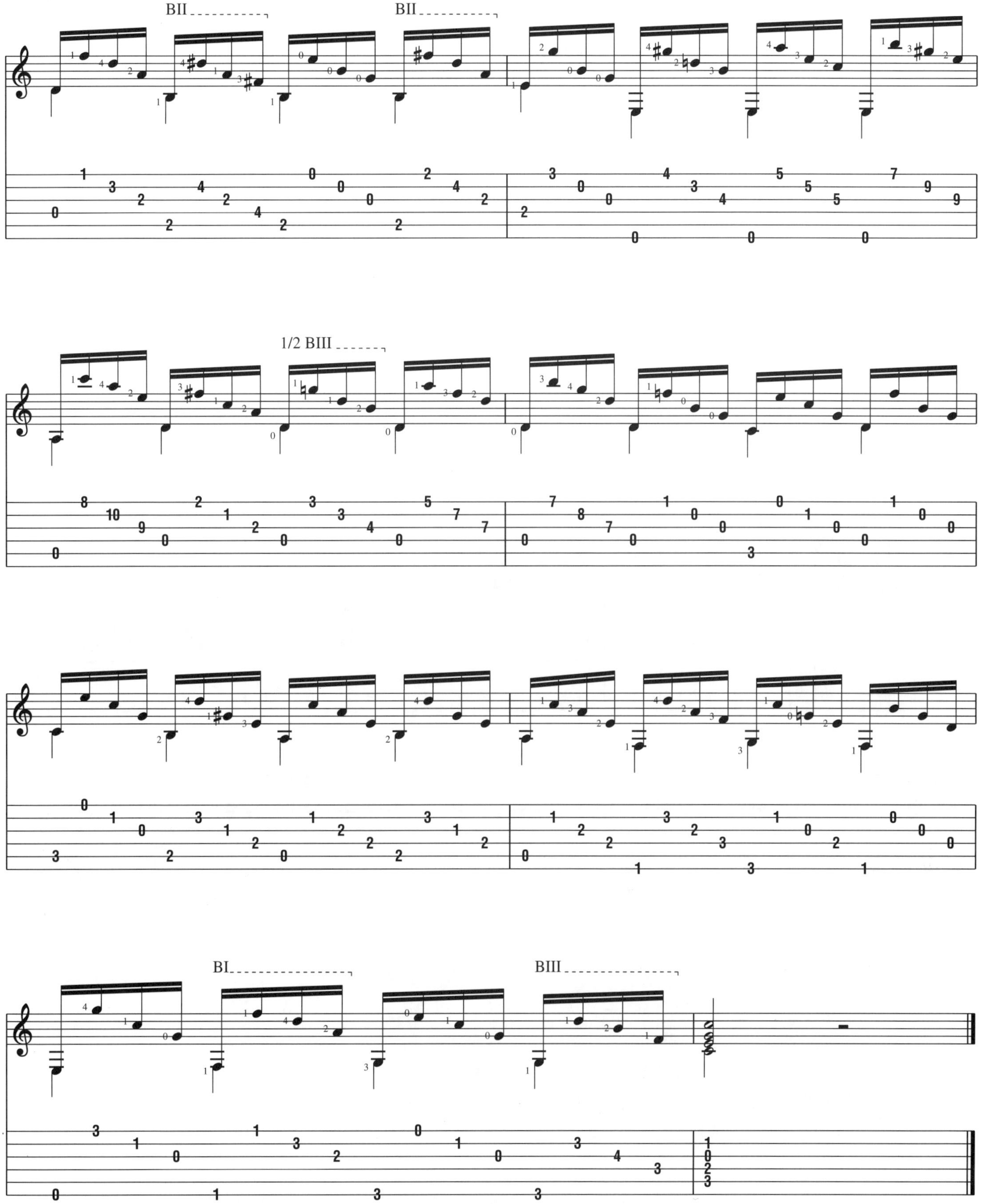
BII
BII
1/2 BIII
BI
BIII

LEFT HAND
The Pre-Crab Exercise

This exercise takes the supported finger exercise one step further: by having *two fingers* moving in opposite directions at the same time. Again, this is a way to develop your left-hand finger independence. While practicing this exercise, focus on the same points as the supported finger exercise:

- Make sure that your left hand and wrist are a natural extension of the forearm.
- The left-hand thumb should be exerting very little if no pressure on the back of the neck.
- Think only of the fingers that are moving, and try not to think about the other fingers that are resting on the third string. (The fingers not moving should be resting *lightly* on the string.)
- Let your fingers move slowly and with precision.
- Concentrate on the motion and direct each movement.

Practice in pairs, then in a full sequence. Begin at the fifth position, but don't be afraid to move this exercise up and down the fingerboard.

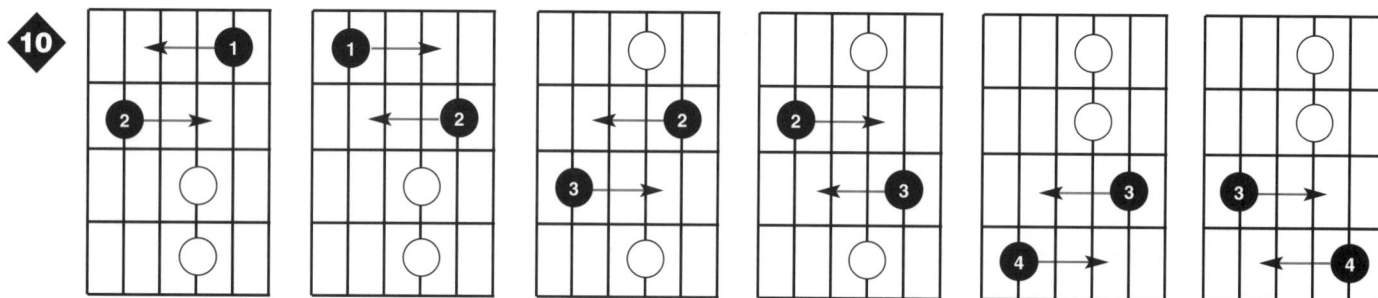

Practice both the supported finger exercise and the pre-crab exercise for several weeks, and then practice just the pre-crab exercise. Time frames are important: Try five-minute practice sessions that include a one-minute break.

By the way, I call this the "pre-crab exercise" because it's a good preparation for the "crab exercise," which we'll learn later.

Lesson 4
RIGHT HAND
Combining Forward and Reverse Arpeggios

There's really nothing new here, as we're just combining the forward and reverse arpeggio patterns that we learned previously. If you've practiced those lessons well, you'll be ready for these more advanced combinations.

Practice the following patterns slowly but with great velocity in your movements. Observe all of the different aspects of playing arpeggios that we've talked about up to this point: the finger touches the string (or plants) an instant before it plucks, the tip segment relaxes slightly, and the attack is quick with a smooth follow-through; then the finger cycles back to play again. All of this must be accomplished in one thought process.

Here's a double-stop arpeggio pattern that requires the thumb and index to pluck together, followed by *m* and *a*.

⑭ Study #2 in E Minor

Dionisio Aguado
(1784-1849)

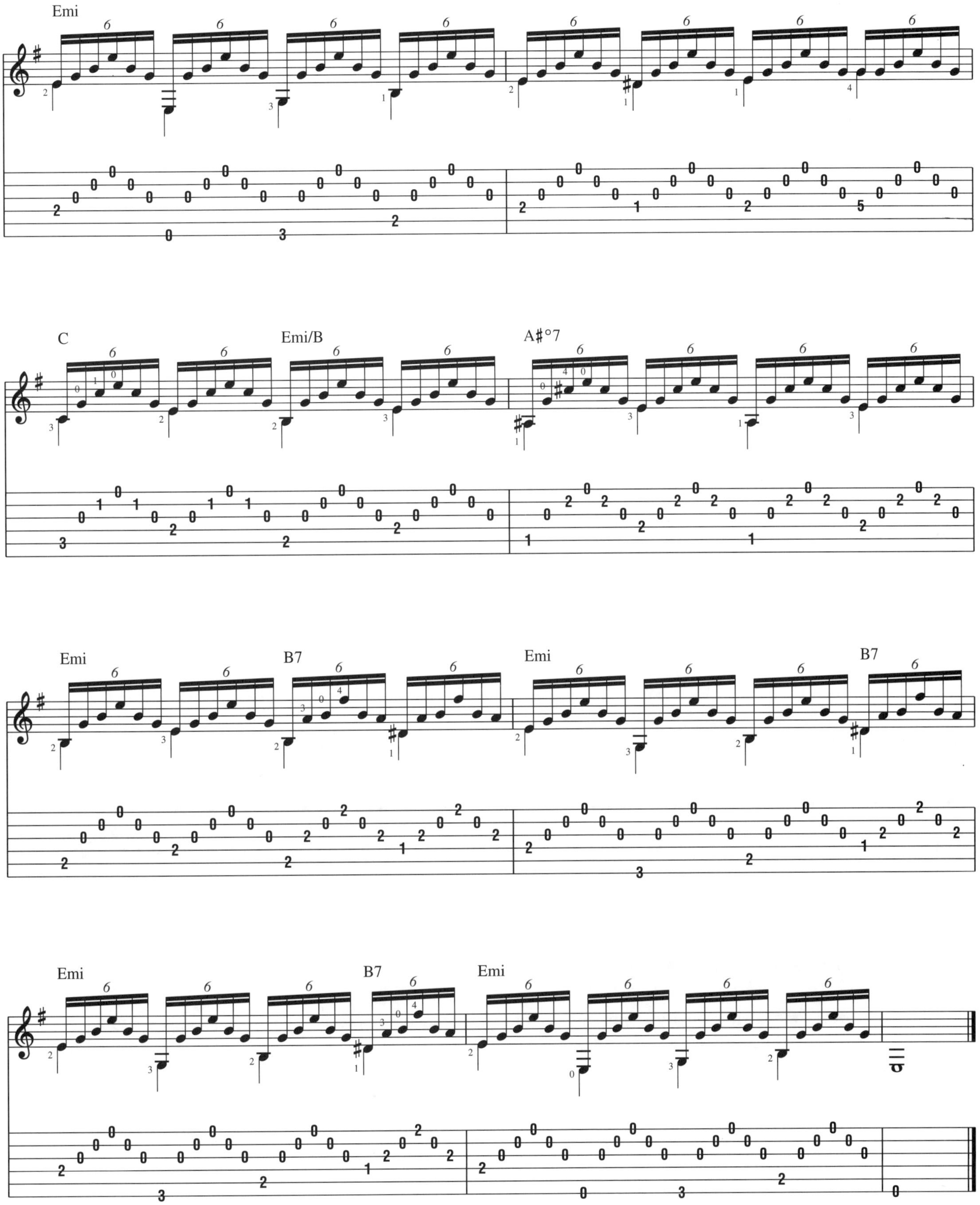
Emi
C
Emi/B
A♯°7
Emi
B7
Emi
B7
Emi
B7
Emi

Lesson 5
RIGHT HAND
Tremolo Technique

Tremolo—the quick repetition of a single note—is one of the most difficult of all the arpeggio techniques. It was developed in the eighteenth and nineteenth centuries and is used today in many different styles of music.

Here are four of the most common tremolo patterns. These can be applied to any progression. Practice them slowly but with great velocity in your movements and a quick release off the string. Strive for an even sound between the notes. Touch each string before you pluck: This will develop an evenness of attack, even though you are stopping the sound of the string. (As you increase your tempo, try not to touch each note in advance.) Practicing slowly in this way will also help you keep the tremolo rhythmically even.

These first two tremolo patterns would be appropriate for a fast tempo song—like "Asturias," a piano work by Isaac Albeniz that is also known by its subtitle "Leyenda." This is one of the most popular classical guitar transcriptions and defines much of the Spanish classical guitar sound:

This next one is a standard classical pattern; it would be appropriate for a piece like Francisco Tarrega's "Recuerdos de la Alhambra." Technique-wise, the classical pattern is probably the most important tremolo to develop. Unfortunately, it is very easy to play unevenly or with a rhythmic gallop. To counter this, we need to practice slowly and accent different parts of the beat. For example, when practicing slowly, try accenting every third note—the note played with the middle finger. This will help even out the sound at faster tempos.

Most flamenco songs are slower than the standard classical tremolo, so they would use the fourth pattern, to make them sound faster:

18 **Flamenco style**

Sustaining or maintaining an even tremolo sound for an entire work is very demanding, which makes this Carcassi study a great place to start. Study #7 combines tremolo in short bursts with combination arpeggio techniques.

19 **Study #7 in A Minor**

Matteo Carcassi

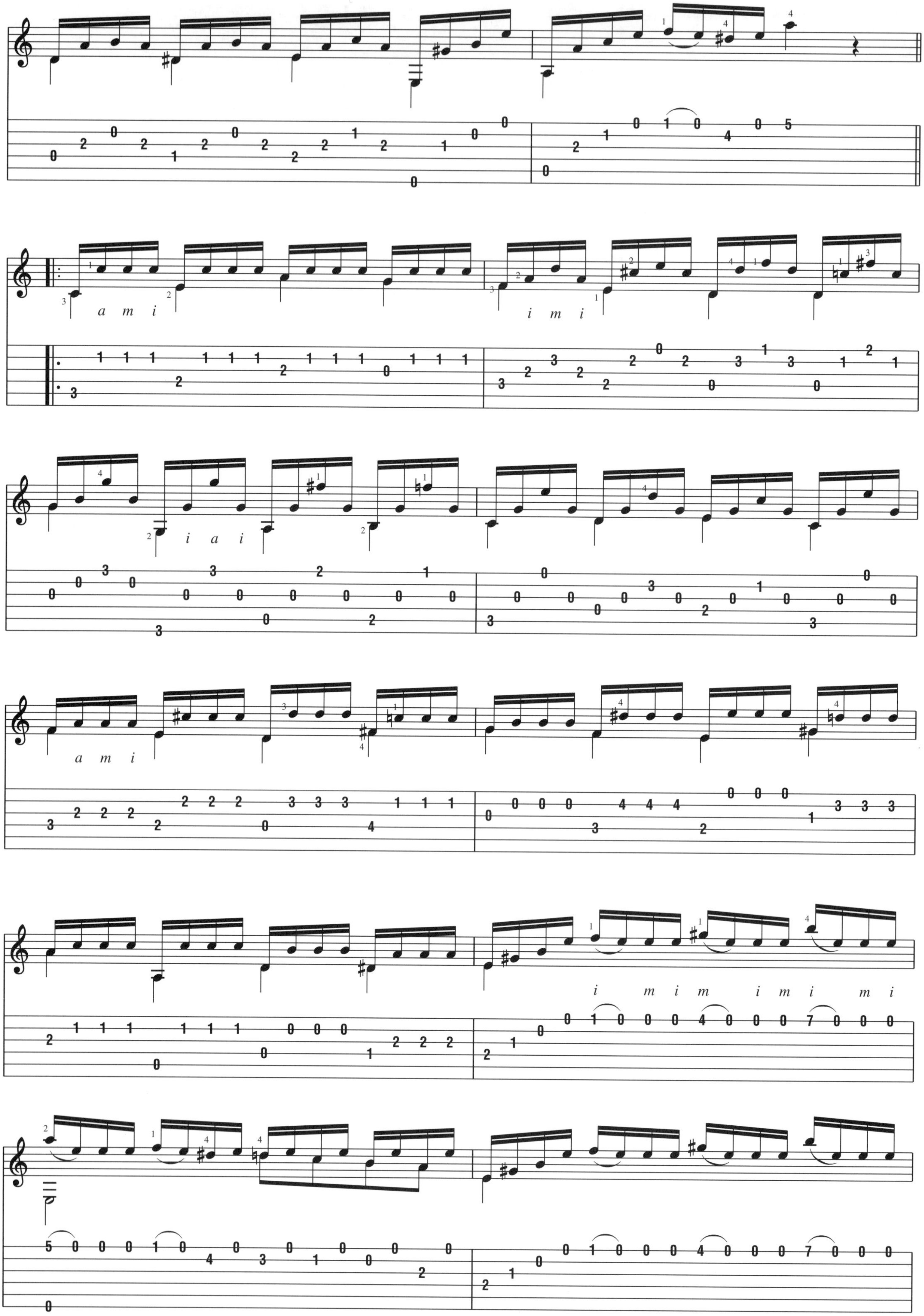
a m i
i m i
i a i
a m i
i m i m i m i m i

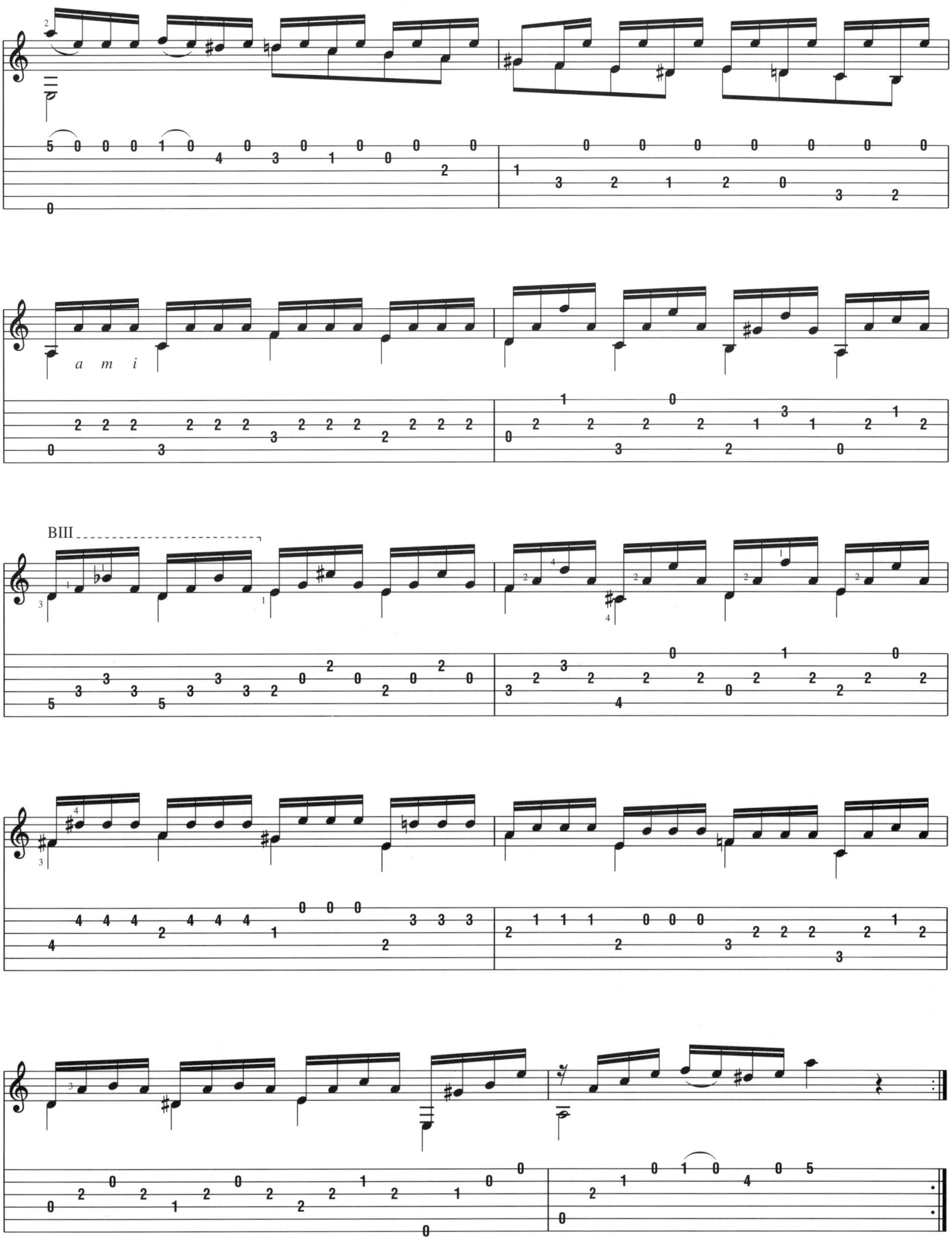
a m i
BIII

LEFT HAND
The Crab Exercise

Here it is! This is one of the best exercises ever created for developing left-hand finger independence. It will eventually replace the supported finger and pre-crab exercises in your daily technique program. Use the same practice techniques outlined for the supported finger exercise, but also think about these concepts:

- Practice legato (connected); don't play the notes short or detached.
- The fingers that are not playing are preparing their next move in advance.

This is a great exercise to play all over the fingerboard; To begin with, start it in the fifth position, and move up. After it is comfortable, move it down the fingerboard to the first position.

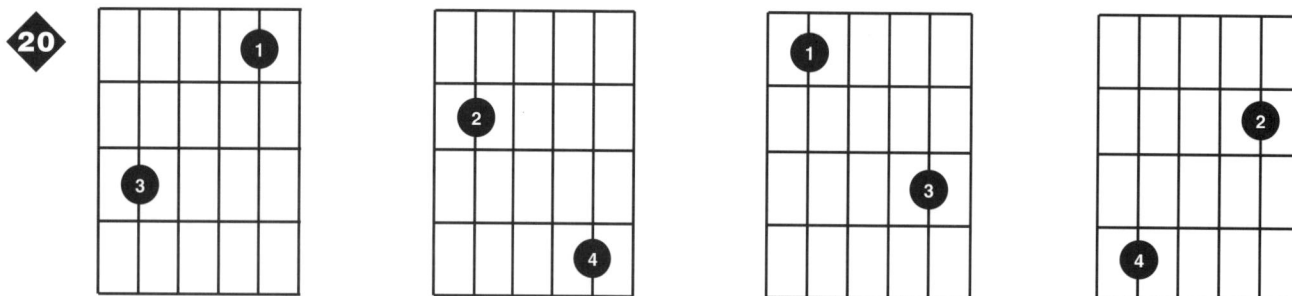

Again, short time frames are very important. This exercise should be practiced no more than five minutes per day. This study, if overpracticed, can produce very tired and sore muscles.

Lesson 6

RIGHT HAND
Thumb Independence

Independence between the thumb and index finger is an important technique to develop because it relates to so many different stylistic fingerstyle applications on the guitar. In most fingerstyle guitar music (especially Atkins/Travis-style alternate bass fingerpicking), the thumb and index finger play very important roles. The exercises below are more advanced right-hand studies for developing independent movement between the thumb and the index finger.

Study #14 is a very tough piece of music to play well. It is one of the few pieces in the classical guitar repertoire where the melody is played entirely by the thumb while the fingers play a broken chord accompaniment pattern. There is also a lot of rhythmic syncopation between the thumb and fingers. Try to hold all the melody notes for their full values. Listen carefully to the audio if you are having trouble with the triplets against the eighth notes.

26 Study #14 in A

Dionisio Agaudo

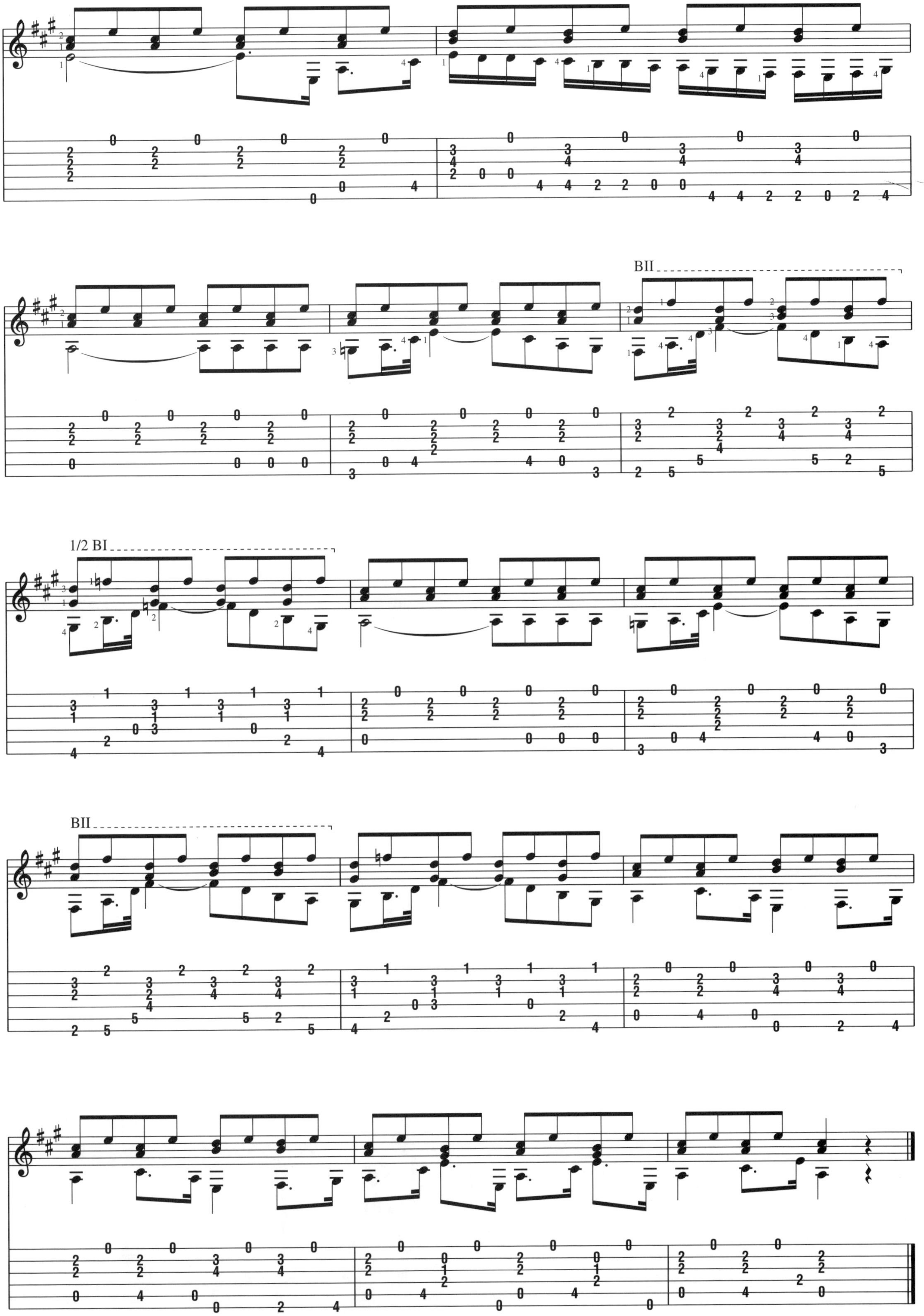
BII
1/2 BI
BII

Walking Bass

Another style that desperately needs thumb independence is fingerstyle jazz. Usually in jazz, chords tend to change on beats 1 and possibly on beat 3 in a common time measure. When you hear guitar players comping behind a soloist, they are usually playing around these two beats. They can place the chord in front of the beat anticipating the chord change, on the beat where the chord change happens, or behind the beat delaying the sound of the change. The bass player, who plays a walking line, as well as the drummer need to play steady time while the guitarist is playing freely.

Play the B♭ blues progression below with the thumb keeping steady time while the fingers play the chords as if you were comping:

- Play the bass line softer than the chords. Use the flesh of the thumb and not the nail.
- Ghost bass notes when possible and when musical. Try pulling off to open strings, creating a rhythmic effect, not a melodic effect.
- Keep the bass line steady while the chords are played in front, behind, or on the beat.
- Watch the fingering. It is a little tricky.

27 B♭ Blues

Lesson 7

RIGHT HAND
P-i Scale Technique

Thumb-and-index scale technique has been around since the Renaissance lute days as a means of performing single-line scale patterns. Today, classical guitarists prefer to alternate the index and middle fingers rather than *p* and *i*. They correctly find that the alternation of *p* and *i* is too uneven for most classical music passages. However, that is exactly the same reason that fingerstyle guitarists love this combination; single-line improvisations in jazz and other popular styles need to sound uneven in order to swing, which calls for the sound of *p* and *i*. As fingerstyle guitarists, we should be able to use many different fingerstyle combinations in many different styles of music.

Work on the following scale-based exercises, alternating between the thumb and index fingers of the right hand. Practice slowly, gradually building your speed while staying relaxed in your right hand. This is still a free stroke technique. Keep your right hand very steady while playing through these scale passages.

28 G major scale, 2nd position

29 C major scale, 2nd position—groups of 3

30 D major scale, 2nd position—groups of 4

31 G major scale, 2nd position—diatonic seventh chords

32 G major triad, 2nd position—upper and lower neighbors

33 G major scale, 2nd position—repeated note pattern

This is an excerpt from one of Bach's violin works, the gigue from Partita #2. It has been changed rhythmically and fingered for the guitar. The fingerings in both the right and left hands are tricky. Alternate between the thumb and index on all eighth notes, except where marked. The piece begins in the fifth position.

If you're having trouble with alternating the thumb and index, go back and spend some more time on the scale exercises.

◆34 Gigue (excerpt)

J.S. Bach

roll 3rd finger

LEFT HAND
Shifting Positions: The Inchworm Technique

Have you ever noticed the way an inchworm moves? It seems to contract and then extend its body to move forward. We will apply this same principle to position shifting. When shifting to a higher position on the fingerboard, bring your left-hand index finger in *towards the middle finger.* This will help your hand to relax just before the shift. Your eye should be focused on the fret or position to which you are shifting. Practice this concept very slowly, making all the moves happen very quickly.

The following chromatic exercise combines position shifting with *p-i* scale technique in the right hand. This is a great exercise to work on for synchronization between the two hands. Keep these points in mind as you practice this exercise:

- When shifting positions, make sure that your fingers are as close together as possible just before each shift. Make each shift as quickly as possible.
- The eyes should be looking at the fret or position to which you are shifting.
- The left-hand thumb should be adding very little pressure and moving with the fingers as they shift up the fingerboard.

35 Chromatic triplets

34

Lesson 8
RIGHT HAND
Three-to-a-String Patterns

Three-to-a-string scale patterns are used by fingerstyle guitarists as a method for getting very quickly from one place on the guitar to another. This technique was first developed by country guitarist Chet Atkins and later copied by jazz fingerstylist Lenny Breau. Subsequently, many pick-style studio guitarists like Tommy Tedesco and Lee Ritenour adopted these scales and inspired many other players to master them. The downside of this technique is that it is not used in classical guitar literature; the attack is too light and uneven in the way the accents fall.

While three-to-a-string patterns are essentially a left-hand shortcut, they correspond to a right-hand pattern of *m-i-p* (or *p-m-i,* when descending). This combination tremolo/arpeggio produces a very light and fast single-note scale type sound that works equally well on electric and classical guitar.

Begin practicing this technique in repeated-note patterns—first in groups of threes, then in groups of fours. Then apply it to various scales. Keep your right-hand position very relaxed. As always, begin slowly. When you get this technique up to speed, it should feel like a tremolo moving across the strings. Consider the following as you practice these exercises:

- Three-to-a-string patterns work only with an effective and well-thought-out fingering for string crossing. The middle finger *(m)* always crosses to the next string when *ascending;* it's the longest finger and reaches upward most easily. The thumb *(p)* always crosses to the next string when *descending;* it is perfectly positioned to change strings going downward.
- Practicing three-to-a-string scales in different rhythmic patterns and cross accents like the tremolo technique helps to even out the sound.
- Anytime you use the thumb with the fingers in a scale pattern, there will be a noticeable change in timbre.

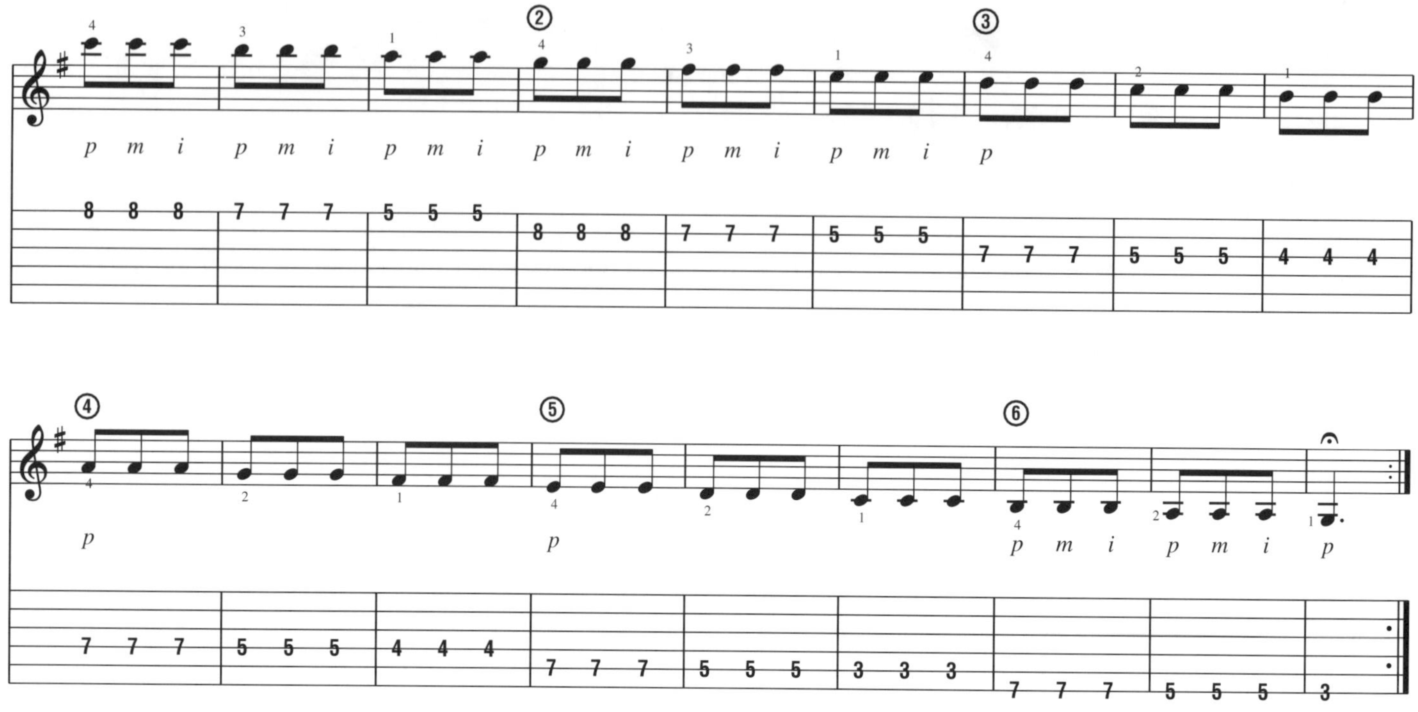

37

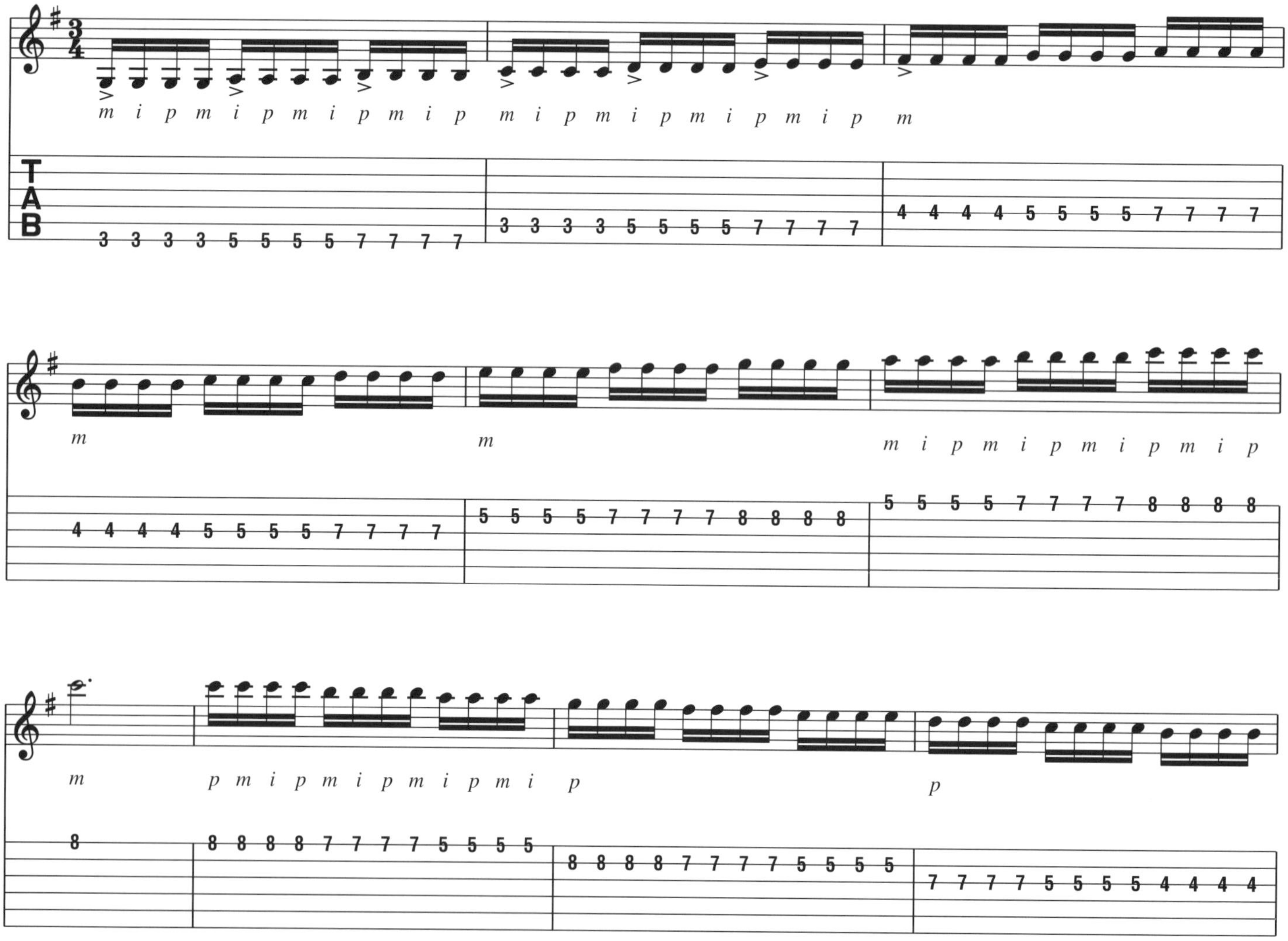

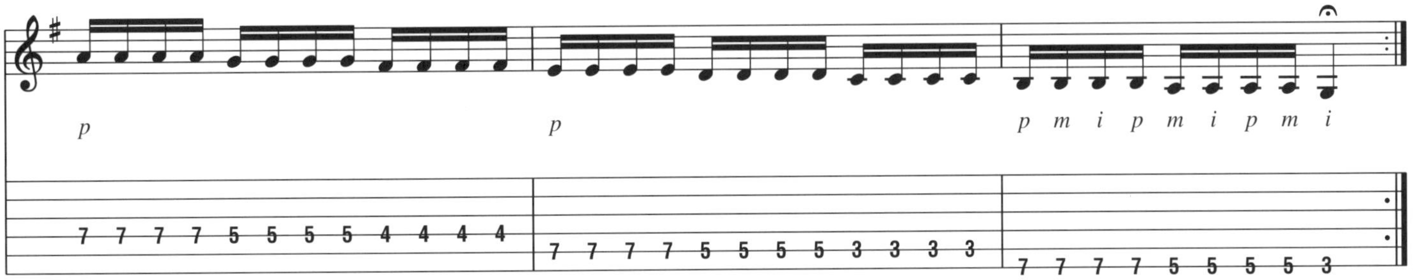

38

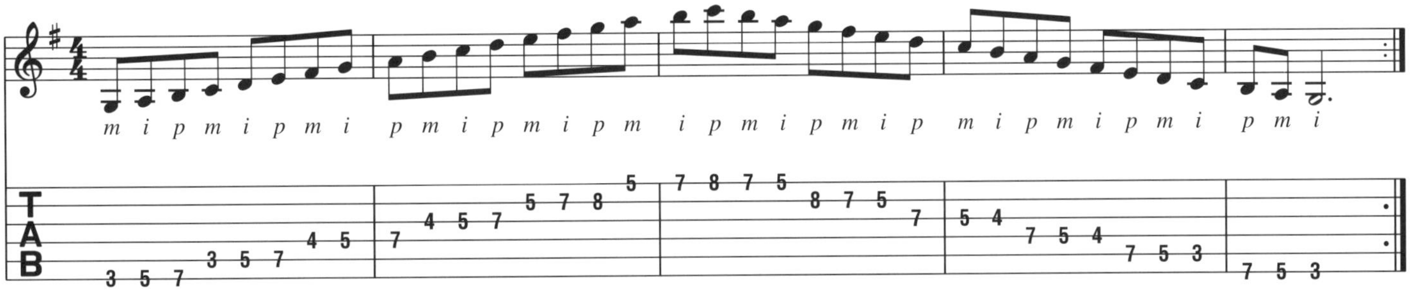

39 **Chromatic triplets** ♩ = 40-200

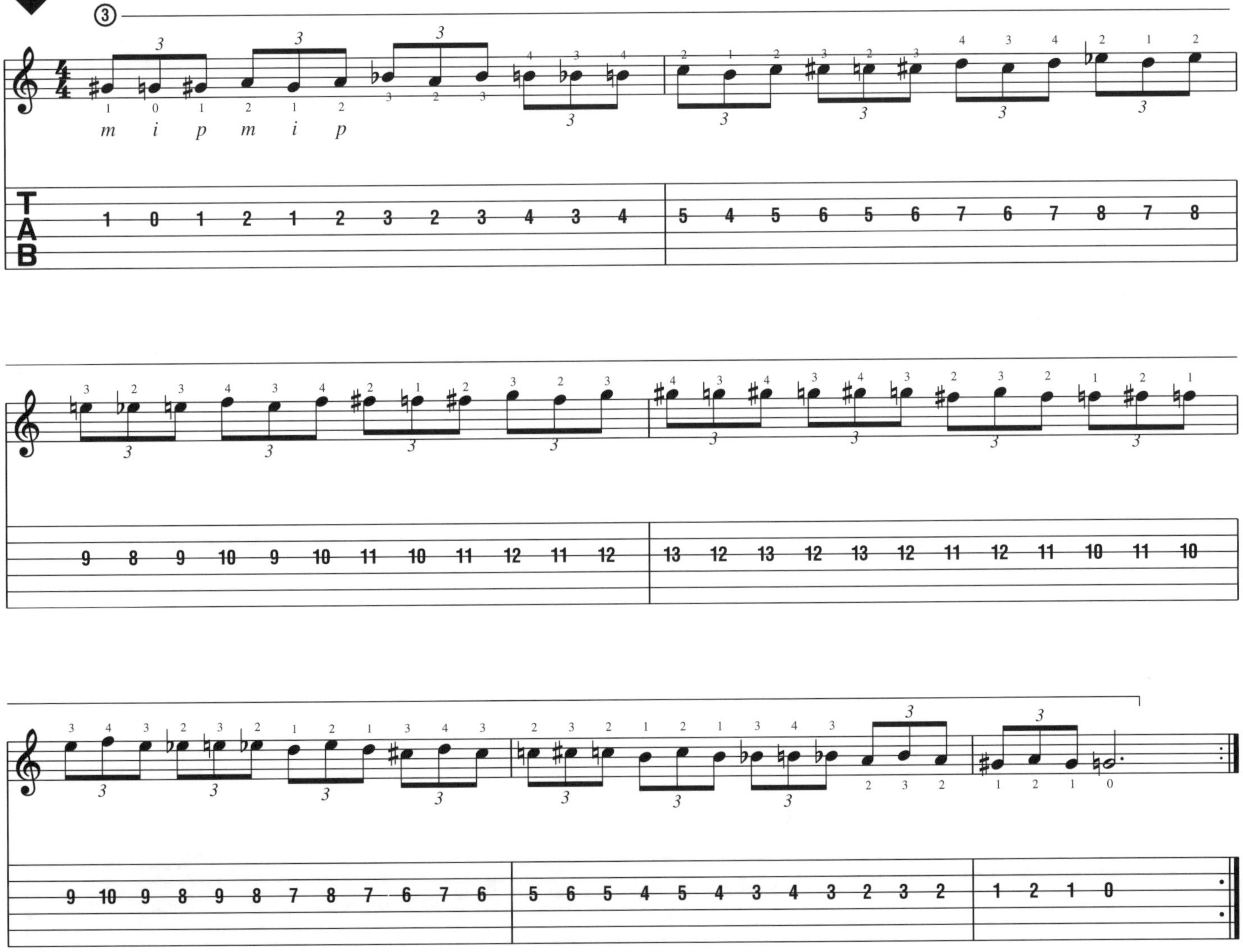

40 Bb diminished scale

41 Chromatic triplets across the fingerboard ascending

42 Chromatic triplets across the fingerboard descending

43 Whole-tone scale

44 Whole-tone scale combining m-i-p and p-i

45 Open-string exercise, third position

LEFT HAND
Chromatic Octaves

"Chromatic octaves" is an exercise developed by the Italian virtuoso Mauro Giuliani in the early nineteenth century. This exercise takes the crab exercise one step further, and the same practice concepts hold true for both studies. If you like these studies, then check out Giuliani's *Studies for the Left Hand.*

As usual, practice this exercise very slowly, making all the movements happen very quickly. Try to keep the following points in mind:

- Make sure that your left hand and wrist are a natural extension of the forearm.
- The left-hand thumb should be adding very little if no pressure.
- Don't play the notes short or detached. Practice legato.
- Be aware of your fingers, and direct your movements in advance. The fingers that are not playing should be preparing.

46 Chromatic octaves

47 Chromatic octaves—variation

Lesson 9
RIGHT HAND
Rest Stroke: The Exchange

The *rest stroke* is a technique used by classical guitarists to help project a melody or bring out a line. Compared to the free stroke, the fingers are kept straighter and allowed to "rest" against the adjacent string after plucking; this creates more volume and a fuller, more rounded tone.

The rest stroke is used primarily on nylon-string classical guitars. I would never use it on an electric, acoustic, or electric-acoustic guitar, as the rnovement of the rest stroke is down and into the next string—their action is typically too light for this heavier attack. Again, most of the time, the rest stroke is used to project single-line melodies or to bring out the top notes of an arpeggio sequence.

preparation

completion

The term *exchange* refers to the exchange of "tension and release" in the right hand that occurs while alternating the index *(i)* and middle *(m)* fingers in a rest stroke. For example, if we played a rest stroke on the third string with our index finger, the index finger would come to rest against the fourth string. We are using tension to keep the finger on the fourth string. The middle finger is relaxed and ready to pluck the third string. At the same time that the middle finger plays its rest stroke, the index finger releases off of the fourth string. Now the middle finger has tension, and the index finger is relaxed and ready to play again. This is the exchange of tension and release between the two fingers.

The release off the string and the return speed have to be the same as the speed of the attack. This is a very important technical point—focus on this at the outset instead of your overall tempo. Most guitarists overlook this exchange, and their scales are very sluggish. Working on a quick exchange now will help you to play very powerful and speedy scales later.

One way to build the return speed of the fingers is to practice staccato scales. The finger that returns also has the job of stopping the string sound. The left hand plays in its normal fashion and doesn't aid in the staccato sound. The goal is to make each note sound as short as possible by making the fingers return as quickly as possible. Remember to relax in between each move. This gives you time to check your previous move and direct your next one. Practice this chromatic exercise slowly and work towards a quick rest stroke exchange between the fingers.

Learning how to effectively switch between rest stroke and free stroke also requires work. The main point to observe is that the wrist position of the right hand is slightly higher with the rest stroke than with the free stroke. The fingers attack the string at the same position. The fingers need to straighten out to execute the rest stroke. Remember, this is a very small but necessary movement. In this next pattern, the first four notes are a forward arpeggio, and the next four notes are a reverse arpeggio—both executed with a free stroke. The last four repeated notes of each measure are a rest stroke exchange between the index (i) and the middle (m) fingers.

Classical guitarists love to turn scale patterns into scale studies. Below is a three-octave E major scale pattern mainly in the fourth and ninth positions. Alternate your index and middle fingers and use rest strokes. Practice slowly, working to achieve an even sound between the index and middle fingers. Notice the open second string that is used for string crossing. This is a classical guitar fingering technique: to use an open string in the middle of a position scale.

Repeated-note scales are also a helpful technique to build speed and exchange of the rest stroke. Use the sixteenth notes to build the exchange speed. Take time to relax on the staccato quarters. You may use other repeated-note patterns that were presented in earlier lessons. Don't force speed. Let it develop naturally.

51 C major repeated-note pattern, 2nd position

52 G major repeated-note pattern, 2nd position

Play all the chords free stroke. Practice all the single-note scales as rest strokes, alternating your index and middle fingers. Play the scales both lightly and rhythmically. Groups of six are hard to feel at first, so be patient. Be aware of your exchange of tension and release while playing this section of the study.

53 Study #20 in A (Part I)

D. Aguado

LEFT HAND
"Thump-to-Pressure"/Balancing the Hands

The "thump-to-pressure" exercise is a simple yet important technique to combine with the rest stroke. We tend to use more pressure than we need to in both hands. This unnecessary build-up of tension affects speed, fluidity, and tone production when playing scales.

With your left-hand index finger resting lightly on the third string, fifth fret, pluck the string with your right-hand index finger (rest stroke) while you slowly add pressure with your left hand. First, the note will sound like a thump. Then, as you add more pressure, you will hear the fret buzz. Then, you will start to hear the pure sound of the note. Stop at this point, and feel how little pressure it actually takes to make a note sound. Be aware of your hand positions.

Now it's time to balance the hands:

• The right-hand thumb on the sixth string should have equal pressure with the left-hand thumb behind the neck of the guitar. This pressure should be very light: the feeling of the fingers touching.
• The left-hand index finger playing the note should have equal pressure with the right-hand index finger resting on the fourth string. This also should be very light.

Now try this same exercise with the right- and left-hand middle fingers. Finally, alternate between the index and middle fingers, with the thumbs on both hands remaining properly balanced. Practice all the rest stroke exercises again as well as Study #20 with this balancing concept in mind.

Lesson 10
LEFT HAND
Legato Technique

Legato is an Italian term meaning "to connect smoothly." Guitarists use hammer-ons and pull-offs (as well as the occasional slide) to make these kinds of connected sounds. Other musicians (flutists, violinists, trumpet players, etc.) think that most classical guitarists have very uneven legatos: The plucked note is louder than the sound of the note hammered on or pulled off to. However, the uneven sound of the legato is perfect for executing jazz and pop music phrasing.

Most classical guitarists don't even realize that their legatos are uneven; they just accept it as part of their sound. To counter this, we need to attack the note lighter and make the legato stronger. The attack to the fingerboard must be very strong and relaxed. For pull-offs, the concept of follow-through is very important: Your fingers must have a uniform curve so that you are playing on your fingertips in order to get a strong sound. In other words, hand positions have to be perfect in order to play strong legatos.

Practice only a few of the different legato exercises listed below on any given day. Play them up and down any string by shifting positions one fret at a time. Use rest strokes, alternating your index and middle fingers in your right hand. Make sure that your hands stay balanced ("thump-to-pressure") while doing these hammer-ons and pull-offs. Be aware of any extra build-up of tension in your left hand. Take time to relax between each series. As always, practice these very slowly, making all the movements happen very quickly.

Try to keep your practicing of these techniques to between 15–30 minutes on any given day.

12th fret

	Hammer-Ons							Pull-Offs					
54	1 2	2 3	3 4	3 4	3 4	3 4	|	4 3	4 3	4 3	4 3	3 2	2 1
55	1 2	1 3	2 3	2 4	3 4		|	4 3	4 2	3 2	3 1	2 1	
56	1 3	1 3	2 4	2 4			|	4 2	4 2	3 1	3 1		
57	1 2 1	2 3 2	3 4 3	3 4 3			|	4 3 4	3 2 3	2 1 2	2 1 2		
58	1 2	1 3	1 4				|	4 3	4 2	4 1			
59	1 4	2 1	3 2	4 3			|	4 1	4 3	3 2	2 1		

This phrase is a great way to develop the evenness of the legato without your right hand.

Flamenco music makes use of every legato technique possible. In the next two examples, lighten up the sound in the right hand to even out the sound of the legato. Most flamenco players will hold the F note on the fourth string, third fret while playing the other hammer-ons and pull-offs that move towards that note. You might try adding a capo to the second or third fret to help if these are tough to play. Many flamenco players use a capo all the time.

This is the second half of the study from Lesson 9. Work this section slowly to get an even sound between the plucked notes and the pull-offs. This whole section should played with free strokes.

63 ◆ Study #20 in A (Part II)

D. Aguado

Lesson 11

RIGHT HAND
Natural and Artificial Harmonics

Harmonics in the classical guitar repertoire are very different from the octave harmonic style and tapping harmonics of the commercial guitarist. In classical music, harmonics usually float above the harmony of the composition. This requires the ability to play a harmonic with the index and ring fingers while at the same time plucking a chord with the thumb and middle fingers. This technique has been known to try the patience of the most accomplished guitarist—so don't get too frustrated on your first try!

Harmonics are usually notated as a diamond-shaped notehead, and sound an octave higher than written. *Natural harmonics* are found at the fifth, seventh, and twelfth frets. Play the following natural harmonics across the twelfth fret using the two different right-hand fingerings indicated (*i-a* and *i-p*). It is important to become comfortable with both fingerings.

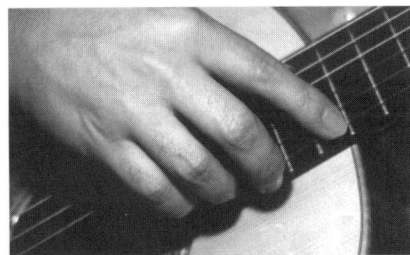

i-a

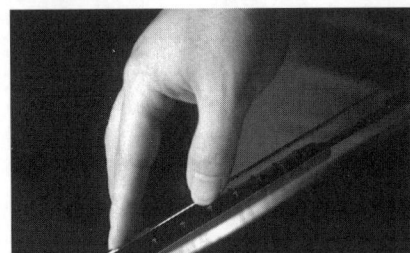

i-p

64 Natural harmonics

Artificial harmonics are formed by fretting the strings with your left hand and sounding the harmonic twelve frets above the fretted note(s) with your right hand. For example, play the following C major scale in the open position. Then lightly touch your right-hand index finger on the same notes twelve frets higher and pluck each octave harmonic with your ring finger. Play them again, this time letting the thumb pluck the harmonic.

65 Artificial harmonics

The next example illustrates the way that harmonics are commonly used in the classical guitar literature: with the harmonic played on top of an accompanying harmony. The thumb plays the lowest note, while the middle finger plays the middle note, and the index and ring fingers play the harmonic on the highest note (the diamond-shaped pitch).

66

67 ◆ Alborada (excerpt)

F. Tarrega

The following examples create a cluster-effect by alternating between harmonics played by the thumb and index finger on a low string with another note played by the ring finger on a higher string. This technique was first developed by country and jazz fingerstyle guitarists but has recently filtered into classical guitar compositions as well.

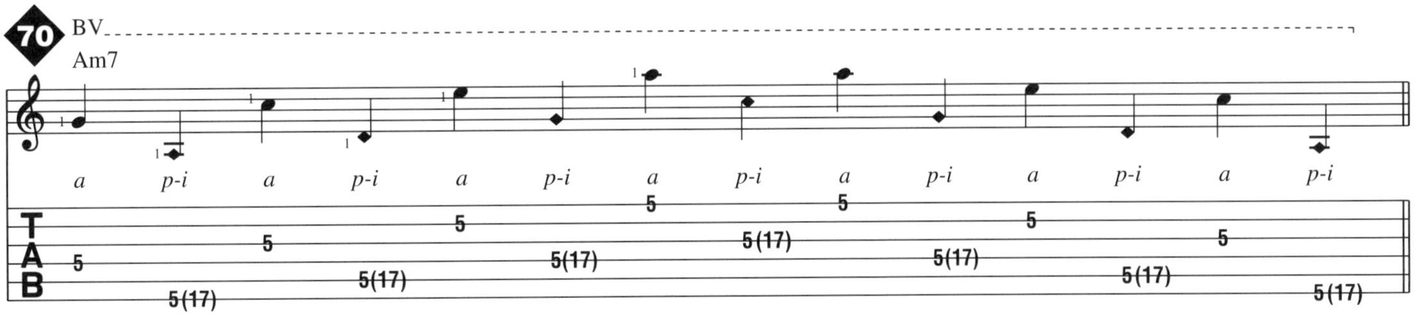
70
BV
Am7
a p-i a p-i a p-i a p-i a p-i a p-i a p-i a p-i
TAB

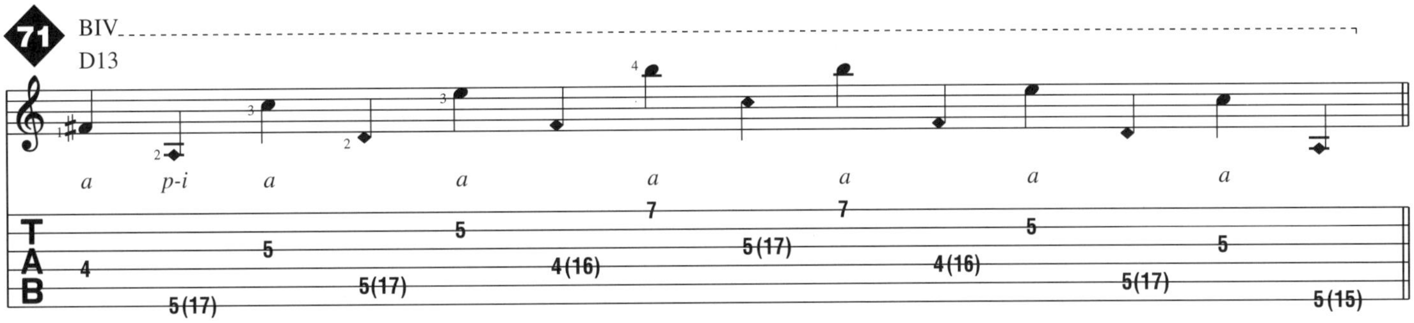
71
BIV
D13
a p-i a a a a a a
TAB

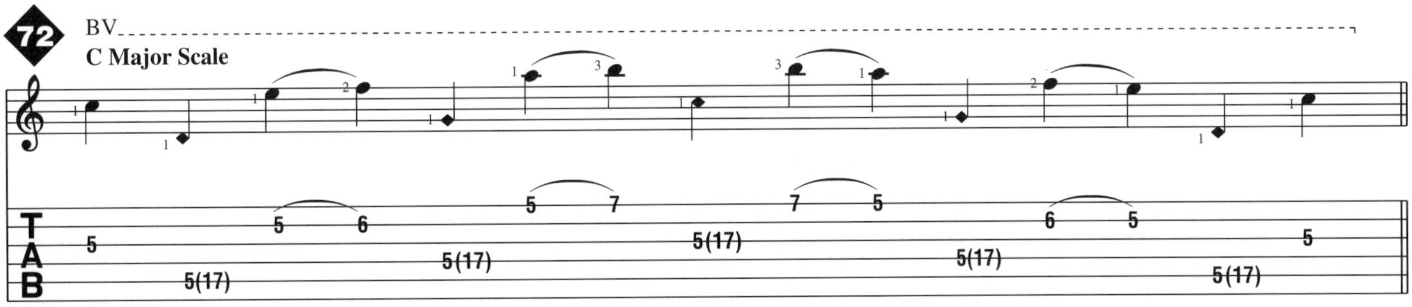
72
BV
C Major Scale
TAB

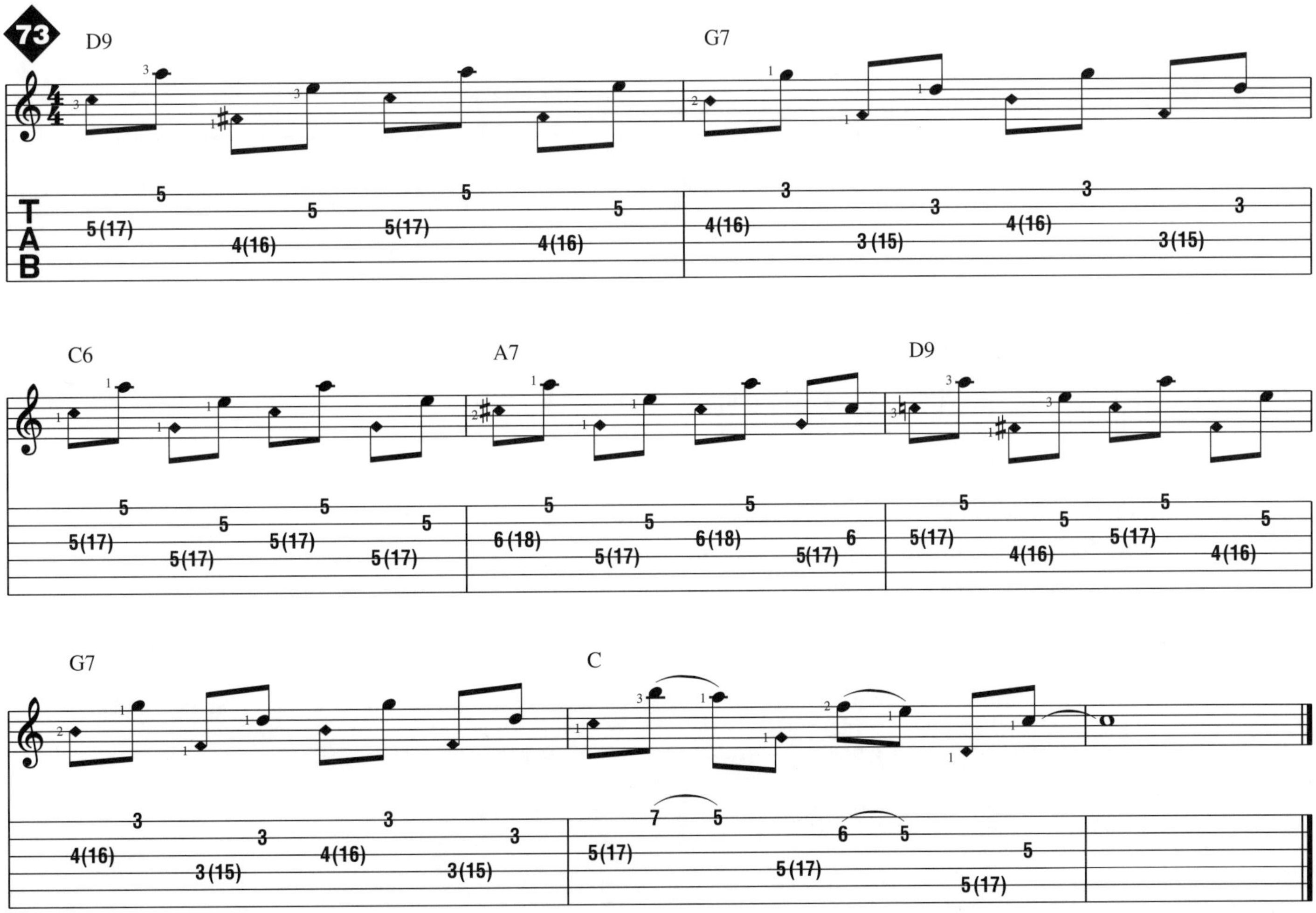
73
D9
G7
TAB
C6
A7
D9
G7
C

Lesson 12
RIGHT HAND
Rasgueado

Rasgueado is the strumming sound that everyone identifies with flamenco music. It is this sound that draws people to the art form. Rasgueados are similar to drum rolls in the sense that they accent the last beat of the strum. While many flamenco guitarists play rasgueados very differently, the only part of the rasgueado that is truly important is this final accented strum; how many attacks you use to get there is irrelevant. (Most flamenco guitarists believe that they play ragueados right and that everyone else plays them wrong—a better way to put it is that most flamenco guitarists do what works best for them!)

Following are five different strum patterns for executing a one-beat rasgueado. Choose whichever feels the most comfortable to you and practice it, or work on them all. You'll notice that rasgueado uses all five fingers of the right hand—even the pinky (indicated in notation as "c" for *cinco* or fifth finger). Also, all five fingers will strum downstrokes, but only the thumb and index finger will strum upstrokes.

Keep the following points in mind as you practice these patterns:

• In the beginning, place your right-hand thumb on the sixth string as an anchor. Don't worry about playing that string for now, even though it is notated to be played.
• Keep your right-hand fingers in a relaxed fist position.
• Strum across the strings lightly and quickly. They should sound (or explode) as one attack.
• Try to extend the finger after the strum (for smooth follow-through).
• Remember that beat 1 is not as important as the accent on beat 2.

Pattern #1 is the four-stroke rasgueado. This is one of the most traditional patterns in flamenco and, because it is executed in even sixteenth notes, it can be used in a variety of situations. Start with the hand in a relaxed fist and strum with your index finger. Then strum with your little finger and bring your index finger back. Then strum with your ring and middle fingers while keeping the little finger extended. When you strum beat 2 with your index finger, all the fingers should be extended.

Pattern #2 is a variation on the four-stroke pattern, used mainly as a punctuation mark for the end of a musical phrase. It is played very quickly with a slight emphasis on beat 2. Experiment with different tempos, trying to get a snare drum effect on the guitar. This pattern is very easy to play sloppy but very difficult to play with precision.

*An up arrow (↑) is the symbol for the downstroke. This may seem backward, but if you think in terms of musical notation, the arrow is pointing from lower notes towards higher notes. The only way to achieve this is with a downstroke on the guitar. Likewise, a down arrow (↓) is the symbol for an upstroke, notes moving from high to low.

Pattern #3 is another variation of the four-stroke rasgueado. It is easier to play because the opening eighth note gives your weaker fingers time to set up. Again, keep your attacks light and articulate. Listen to the CD; I vary the rhythm of the sixteenth-note triplets.

Pattern #4 uses the thumb with down- and upstrokes. Rotate your forearm from your elbow while doing this strum. Keep your wrist very loose. This is a popular rasgueado for punctuating the ends of phrases in a rumba. (More on this later.)

Pattern #5 is often called the five-stroke rasgueado. Make sure that the index upstroke is even with the other attacks. This is a very difficult pattern at first, but you will find a lot of possibilities with it.

Warning: Overpracticing rasgueados can be hazardous to your health. Training your fingers to perform rasgueados is very difficult; you are basically working with muscles that you have never used to play the guitar, and these muscles will get very sore very quickly. Practice rasgueados in short time frames, and be aware of what your fingers are telling you while practicing. Tired, sore, aching muscles are your body's way of telling you that you have practiced too much and it is time to rest. Consistent practicing over a period of months will build the stamina that you will need to play flamenco. Remember how hard it was to play your first F chord?

Let's apply the previous patterns to this progression in the style of Farruca. On the fourth example, use your wrist to strum the first measure.

Flamenco Accents and Articulations

The Golpe

The word *golpe* means "to tap." Flamenco guitarists use the golpe to imitate the sounds of the heel of flamenco dancers. The ring finger of the right hand is used to tap the top of the fingerboard. There are only three combinations for using the golpe.

- Tap with the ring finger without a strum, producing a rhythmic effect.
- Tap with the ring finger in combination with a downstroke of the index finger.
- Tap with the ring finger in combination with a downstroke of the thumb.

Golpes can be marked on the manuscript with an accent mark (>) or the symbol G . Make sure that you have a tap plate applied to your guitar, or your instrument will take on a "Willie Nelson" look.

The Apagado

The word *apagado* means "to silence." Flamenco guitarists use the apagado to enhance the sounds of the accents in flamenco. The fourth finger of the left hand is brought down across the strings to give the effect of the accented staccato. Apagados can be marked on the manuscript with a staccato mark (.) or the symbol A .

Practice the patterns on page 54 again, using golpes on beats 1 and 3 of the first measure and beat 1 of the second measure. Use the apagado on beats 3 and 4 of measure 2. Play it loose and use different combinations of these articulations. Do not use these articulations with the fourth example. There will be other ways to accent these lines.

Rumba Patterns

The rumba is the most often used, abused, and imitated rhythm in flamenco music. The most important element of the rumba to remember is "never strum on beat 3." The right hand uses two percussive techniques with the rumba: the golpe on beat 1 and the *slap* (a right-hand form of the apagado) on beat 3. The left-hand apagado will also be used on beat 3. The two percussive attacks on beats 1 and 3 are the guitarist's way of imitating the bongo. Tempos for the rumba range from very slow (rumba/bolero) to very fast cut-time.

A very traditional rumba pattern. Beat 3 can be attacked with a right-hand slap or a left-hand apagado. Work the tempo up to a cut-time feel. Also, as a variation, play on the lower strings on the first half of the measure and on the upper strings on beats 3 and 4.

A rhythmic variation on the previous example. Vary your tempos.

Play this example with a slower four feel. The slap is made by tapping your knuckles on the fingerboard, producing a snare effect.

A typical turnaround for an up-tempo rumba.

This study uses chord voicings that take advantage of open strings. Practice changing between patterns 1 and 2. Practice at tempos set between common and cut time.

92 Blue Rumba

About the Author

For the past twenty years, David Oakes has taught guitar at four different universities as well as at the renowned Musicians Institute in Hollywood, California. Currently, in addition to teaching his MI curriculum, he holds the position of part-time lecturer in the Studio Jazz Guitar department at the University of Southern California. At both schools, his focus is on building classical/fingerstyle guitar techniques and developing music reading literacy among students studying commercial guitar styles.

David himself has studied with many great classical guitarists—including Pepe Romero, Juan Serrano, Jesus Silva, and Jonathan Marcus—and with other fine guitarists in genres ranging from jazz to fingerstyle to flamenco. He graduated with a B.M. in classical guitar performance in 1978 from the North Carolina School of the Arts.

If you have any comments about this book, please feel free to e-mail the author at oakes@almaak.usc.edu.

MUSICIANS INSTITUTE

Press

Musicians Institute Press

is the official series of Southern California's renowned music school, Musicians Institute. **MI** instructors, some of the finest musicians in the world, share their vast knowledge and experience with you – no matter what your current level. For guitar, bass, drums, vocals, and keyboards, **MI Press** offers the finest music curriculum for higher learning through a variety of series:

ESSENTIAL CONCEPTS
Designed from MI core curriculum programs.

MASTER CLASS
Designed from MI elective courses.

PRIVATE LESSONS
Tackle a variety of topics "one-on-one" with MI faculty instructors.

FOR MORE INFORMATION, SEE YOUR LOCAL MUSIC DEALER, OR WRITE TO:

HAL•LEONARD®
CORPORATION

7777 W. BLUEMOUND RD. P.O. BOX 13819 MILWAUKEE, WI 53213

Prices, contents, and availability subject to change without notice. Some products may not be available outside of the U.S.A.

GUITAR

Advanced Scale Concepts & Licks for Guitar
by Jean Marc Belkadi
Private Lessons
00695298 Book/CD Pack $12.95

Basic Blues Guitar
by Steve Trovato
Private Lessons
00695180 Book/CD Pack $12.95

Creative Chord Shapes
by Jamie Findlay
Private Lessons
00695172 Book/CD Pack $7.95

Diminished Scale for Guitar
by Jean Marc Belkadi
Private Lessons
00695227 Book/CD Pack $9.95

Guitar Basics
by Bruce Buckingham
Private Lessons
00695134 Book/CD Pack $14.95

Guitar Hanon
by Peter Deneff
Private Lessons
00695321 . . . . $9.95

Guitar Soloing
by Dan Gilbert & Beth Marlis
Essential Concepts
00695190 Book/CD Pack $17.95

Harmonics for Guitar
by Jamie Findlay
Private Lessons
00695169 Book/CD Pack $9.95

Jazz Guitar Chord System
by Scott Henderson
Private Lessons
00695291 . . . . $6.95

Jazz Guitar Improvisation
by Sid Jacobs
Master Class
00695128 Book/CD Pack $17.95

Modern Approach to Jazz, Rock & Fusion Guitar
by Jean Marc Belkadi
Private Lessons
00695143 Book/CD Pack $12.95

Music Reading for Guitar
by David Oakes
Essential Concepts
00695192 . . . . $16.95

Rhythm Guitar
by Bruce Buckingham & Eric Paschal
Essential Concepts
00695188 . . . . $16.95

Rock Lead Basics
by Nick Nolan & Danny Gill
Master Class
00695144 Book/CD Pack $14.95

Rock Lead Performance
by Nick Nolan & Danny Gill
Master Class
00695278 Book/CD Pack $16.95

Rock Lead Techniques
by Nick Nolan & Danny Gill
Master Class
00695146 Book/CD Pack $14.95

BASS

Arpeggios for Bass
by Dave Keif
Private Lessons
00695133 . . . . $12.95

Bass Fretboard Basics
by Paul Farnen
Essential Concepts
00695201 . . . . $12.95

Bass Playing Techniques
by Alexis Sklarevski
Essential Concepts
00695207 . . . . $14.95

Grooves for Electric Bass
by David Keif
Private Lessons
00695265 Book/CD Pack $12.95

Music Reading for Bass
by Wendy Wrehovcsik
Essential Concepts
00695203 . . . . $9.95

Odd-Meter Bassics
by Dino Monoxelos
Private Lessons
00695170 Book/CD Pack $14.95

KEYBOARD

Music Reading for Keyboard
by Larry Steelman
Essential Concepts
00695205 . . . . $12.95

R & B Soul Keyboard
by Henry J. Brewer
Private Lessons
00695327 . . . . $16.95

Salsa Hanon
by Peter Deneff
Private Lessons
00695226 . . . . $10.95

DRUM

Brazilian Coordination for Drumset
by Maria Martinez
Master Class
00695284 Book/CD Pack $14.95

Chart Reading Workbook for Drummers
by Bobby Gabriele
Private Lessons
00695129 Book/CD Pack $14.95

Working the Inner Clock for Drumset
by Phil Maturano
Private Lessons
00695127 Book/CD Pack $16.95

VOICE

Sightsinging
by Mike Campbell
Essential Concepts
00695195 . . . . $16.95

ALL INSTRUMENTS

An Approach to Jazz Improvisation
by Dave Pozzi
Private Lessons
00695135 Book/CD Pack $17.95

Encyclopedia of Reading Rhythms
by Gary Hess
Private Lessons
00695145 . . . . $19.95

Going Pro
by Kenny Kerner
Private Lessons
00695322 . . . . $19.95

Harmony & Theory
by Keith Wyatt & Carl Schroeder
Essential Concepts
00695161 . . . . $17.95

Lead Sheet Bible
by Robin Randall
Private Lessons
00695130 Book/CD Pack $19.95

WORKSHOP SERIES

Transcribed scores of the greatest songs ever!

Blues Workshop
00695137 . . . . $19.95

Classic Rock Workshop
00695136 . . . . $19.95

R & B Workshop
00695138 . . . . $19.95